BREATHING WATER
BY RED MEDUSA

Cover design by @tg_grfx
Copyright © RED MEDUSA 2022
All rights reserved

For my children, Fertz and Yémi

BREATHING WATER

EGGUN (Ancestors) 6
STRIPPER..8
*ASTERIX..11
LITTLE GREEN FRIEND..13
THEM VS U.S..17
BREONNA, SANDRA, SARAH...21
THESE HANDS 24
HUMAN 27
HERE TO STAY (Written with Osman Yuzefzada) 30
FOR OLOKUN 33

EGGUN (Ancestors)

My Godmother told me
that your name is Eggun

it is you
who I've felt surround me when life rendered me naked
and exposed to the elements
and it is you who sends those signs and wonders
symbols and numbers
times and feathers and feelings
you who bless me with dreams
and visions of what will come
should I will it

as a child
I always knew that you guided my steps
like that day you told me not to take mum's spare change
and spared me some licks
and the day you sent me right when friends advised to go left
I could have been shot
but went home instead
you tug at the pit of my gut
and I move without question
because you have never let me down
your presence is visceral
felt inside and out

your legacy is seen in my mother's eyes
tones heard in Nanas voice
soul present in her Barbadian food
memories of you wash over me in the waters
you are channeled through my words

and honored through my actions
I live because you live
and you live on because I live

so humbly and fiercely
these feet tread the ground you walked upon
strengthened by your stories and led by your light
armed with the knowledge that your blood runs through my veins
Black excellence
Black greatness
expressed through my DNA
remind me not to be afraid
I am safe
in your embrace I am safe

I walk the path
you show me the way
and in return your spirits will be elevated by candlelight
until my day becomes night
and I am returned home to you
you are remembered in all that I do

Marefefun Eggun!

STRIPPER

This woman
is not ashamed to admit

that
I really

like to strip

and bask in the momentary pleasure that sneaks up on me
when feeling my heavy knit dress
slip away from my bodies curvaceous grip

the satisfying sound it makes
as it lands on the floor with a thud
feeling the cold crisp air
licking my skin
as if it had been eagerly waiting for me to come in
wearing nothing
but lace and audacity

when I'm done with performing acceptable femininity
and desire to purge myself of identities that no longer fit
layers of fabric and make up are willingly shed
so when I undress and sacrifice my body
upon the altar of the lens
cycles that reinforce the illusion of conformity
are exiled to remain in my past
and I indulge in forming a future with my flesh

one that rejects social acceptance
and offers visual prayers of thanks
to the me who exists on a higher frequency

to She
who gives less fucks than a nun
she whose agenda is to create, disrupt and have fun
and She
who is smiled upon by Ancestors
who possess the same blissful lust for rebellion

and my rebellion
takes place in full sight of those
who would imprison my spiritual revolution in clothes

I'm fortunate to not have to hide under the covers of darkness to
practice my faith in myself
so, I won't

this sirens' imagery will have religious people praying for my soul
so let them pray

whilst I worship at the temple of me
leaving offerings of endless legs
bountiful breasts
and all of the joys of this unbridled Goddess
for the entire world to see

because, in my nakedness
I proclaim myself to be

holy

an embodiment of the word of God

and

a most delicious kind of blasphemy...

*ASTERIX

I am not an *asterisk
an afterthought
something   'other', that's a little bit different
a blank space
on your form
where my Black is not the norm
I do not represent the spaces between B A M and E
an ethnicity with no name

I am not an *asterisk
I am not a "by the way"
or a covert way to say that I do not fit into your prescribed
d i v i s i v e
European ideals of false supremacy
I am not an outlier
I am not outside of anything
if anything
I am the All in everything
I am that which you say does not exist
I am not an *asterisk

I am not
the acceptably light Black woman you employ
to prove that your organisation is not
racist
an embodied 'get out clause' to meet the quota
I am not your equal opportunities promoter
I am not your poster girl
for how much you say you help the poor
or the Blacks
or the Browns

I am not your 'one Black friend'
I am not your office clown
I am not your foot-in-the-door to Black culture
my presence does not give you permission to speak to me in patois

I cannot be summed up in biro
in a boring white box, ticked
I am not Black – Other
I am not Mixed – Other
I am the sum of my ancestral mothers
I am the strength of ALL of my brothers

I am not an *asterisk

LITTLE GREEN FRIEND

It suppressed my aggression
my anger and depression
making a cruel world disappear into puffs of sweet smoke

Painful childhood memories of
the desperate need for a mother's love
an absent fathers' hugs
and not fully being able to comprehend who and what I was
were expelled with every exhalation
temporarily smudged out of my mind

bags of illegal escapism
were supplied by a hundred different dealers
though I never bought the weed they sold
I purchased a fleeting freedom
a moment of creative peace
or hours of meaningless laughter
followed by a heavy, dreamless sleep

I cherished this substance that helped me to forget those things
that tormented me
smoking it to free my mind of stress
to halt the raging waves behind my eyes
to permit myself a moment of wanton selfishness
where I could abandon the body that anchored me to this painful
existence
and exchange it for an emotionless daydream

I blended into the beige of my smoker's corner
unable to comprehend the depth of feelings I was swimming in
drowning in an ocean of unaddressed trauma

a smokescreen providing me with the shelter I'd looked for my whole life
but it was always temporary
as highs plunged into new lows

every other night
I'd walk to the closest payphone
usually at around one in the morning
and with every ring of the line, I'd grow impatient until he answered
then I'd stay up for as long as it took
waiting for the doorbell to ring
becoming less fussed about whether the dealer would bring buds or dust
as long as he brought me something
it wouldn't matter that I hadn't eaten in a week
because nothing made me feel weaker than having to feel everything
I just wanted to breathe without crying
to be without trying
and smoking weed
made it okay to not care
allowing me to just
sit there

believe me when I say that it's a space that's hard to leave
and it calls you back whenever survival feels too heavy a burden
I mean
all you have to do is roll up
light up
kick back
and be swept away into a purple haze
where you can float on clouds of smoke for days
until you are washed up onto realities stony beaches
hungry, alone and depleted

wanting once more to go offshore
it's the most toxic of relationships and yet
to it I always return
to the familiar smell of burning herbs and rizla papers
that comforting sting on the back of the throat
and then the calm
before the storm every addict knows approaches

I take it right down to the roach
every time
hoping this time will be my last
but my past won't leave me alone
and this hostile world has never felt like home
so for as long as I have to wear a mask
this beautiful visual lie
that convinces everybody that I'm doing fine
I'll stay lit
craving freedom
bent on lightness
devoted to ignorance and to bliss
hooked on freedom of expression
vivid colours
and deep sleep

until poverty and injustice no longer dictate
the terms of my life
and life grants me permission to live
I'll smoke because it provides me with the comfort
that a life of limitations cannot give
it settles my shattered nerves and dreams
which are reimagined and channeled through my poetry
the prickly bitterness of my disappointment in society
becomes a distant memory
and in that space, there is clarity

in that moment, I am free
prison is worth the risk
to momentarily witness my inner scenery change
from the sooty grey of a British winter
into the candy floss pink bloom of a cherry tree

and if I had been given half of the opportunities my peers had in their adolescence
my adulthood wouldn't look like a deadly dance between lung cancer and encroaching criminality
weed wouldn't be a key to the gateway of my sanity
and I wouldn't be locked into this relentless cycle
of dependency
on my little green friend
who met me on the stairs of my estate at fourteen
who has stood by me through by my losses and wins
clean into my thirties

maybe I'll give up in my forties
but I like this so-called dirty habit
so, there you have it
my truth
the story behind my problematic use
and if I gave it up
I would give up
and wouldn't be here talking to you

I'll probably return to purchase that fleeting freedom
because nothing makes me feel weaker
than feeling everything
this substance shields my soul from life's torments
and this poem is my proof

THEM VS U.S.

alive at a time
where the right to govern my body has been snatched from me
by powerful men in high places

men
who have never seen my face

men
who have never bore down to bare children

never tore
never bled
never breastfed
are never going to face death giving birth

these psychopaths
who claim, rape and destroy our mother earth
now claim, rape and force us into motherhood against our will
millions of young girls' futures will perish under the pretense
of protecting lives that don't exist
justified by an archaic religious doctrine
that legitimises the making of our wombs
into political and physical battlefields
where they plow our flesh and plant their seeds against our will
and force the growth and birth of lives
as disposable as the cheap labour and clothes extracted from our
sisters in the global south.

disposable
because those that are forced to raise them will no doubt
be poor

Black
and Brown

we are made to subsidise the state with the bodies it needs
to continue its greedy, capitalist, policies.
we are terrorised into providing an endless supply of lives to be
sent to work
in factories, to war, and to exist at the fringes of society
where a militarised police force plucks them from the streets
and throws them into cells
which feed bottomless private interests
and coverts the value of our flesh
into paid employment and shiny new prisons
whilst incriminating the women who said 'no'

they said no to forced birth
deepening poverty and male extortion
and for that
they will pay with their bodies or their freedom
either way
they have fashioned for us a cage of our wombs
one we can't escape from
unless we are to rip our insides out

and by we
I am not talking about wealthy, conservative women
who can buy their way out of a country
that refuses to put formula on the shelves of its stores
for the babies we will be forced to bear
I'm not talking about right wing
civilisational feminists
that claim to be on the side of all women
whilst clambering for scraps from the blood-stained tables of
patriarchal power

we does not mean 'we'
it means Us

the invisible
racialised
minoritized
sexualised women
that clean your toilets, offices, stations
care for your aging bodies and dying relatives
feed and deliver food to neighborhoods we cannot afford to live in
make and sell clothes we cannot afford to purchase

we
who work in industries your husbands would never tell you that
they 'invest' in...
we
who raise your children for less than minimum wage while you
pursue careers and dreams
we dare not dream about now
we
who are excluded from spaces where our bodily autonomy, race
and class
are the topic of conversation

it is us
who have been designated as the fleshy machinery
and victims of deadly necropolitics
whose screams are heard in ghettos and backstreet abortion clinics

it is us
who are forced to flood the care system with the children we never
wanted
our bodies
will occupy morgues and mental asylums

marked forever as asylum seekers in our own lands
as we attempt to escape a precarious existence
fashioned by heartless white, male hands

we will bleed out
we will suffer
give birth
or beg to be sterilised in the rebirth of a fascist state
where eugenics dictates who gets to live and who gets to die

and I sit here
looking hard at the face of my baby daughter
wondering what f*cked up future awaits her

I sit
with tears and rage flooding the brown of my eyes
sick to my stomach
almost out of hope, out of prayers and out of peace
pleading with the powers that created me

what will it take if not this
to give us the reasons we need to resist?

what will it take if not this
to give us the reasons we need to resist?

what

will it take

if not this

to give us the reasons we need to resist?

BREONNA, SANDRA, SARAH…

Sleep is an escape, reserved for the dead
every breath a deep sigh forced out of a tight chest

I can't breathe

and I didn't resist arrest
but they'll say

"oh, she did
she abused drugs and neglected her kids"

then they'll spit on my character and dance on my grave
post an angry picture of my face
and insist "all lives matter!"
when my sisters scream

"Say her name!"

that undercover Klan member will get away with murder
that undercover fed will surely kill again
next time in a police cell

a rape
a beating
a hanging

and/no

it will be a suicide
because

"She was unstable

unable to drive a vehicle with a broken brake light
and upon confrontation she put up a fight
she had it coming!
she challenged my authority"

when I only dared to look him directly in the eye

they'll say I had an attitude
and no respect for law and order

"She was insubordinate
strong
uncontrollable
and had a mental health disorder"

imagine if I had
Imagine how quickly I'd be picked up
tasered
restrained
locked up and locked in with rapists in uniform
left for dead
found cold on the floor in the morning

as if I was nothing
and never existed

maybe there will be brief mention in the news of some girl called Breonna

Sandra

Sarah

perhaps a protest once they've suffocated another one of my brothers
maybe I'll be a hashtag buried in a million tweets about him

maybe my murder will be relevant
for a short time at least
before this beast goes after my daughter
my sister
my cousin
my mother
my niece

another Black woman
invisible in life and death
another Black woman obscured in the background

will I be her?

will they rage and riot and burn buildings down to their bones?

will they check on my children now they are alone?

will they say my name when I'm framed as a terrorist?

will they speak truth to power when lies are spat from my killers' lips?

will my brothers storm the cities and paint the streets red?

will the only time I mattered be when I am dead?
will the only time I mattered be when I am dead?

THESE HANDS

I have opened my eyes
to find myself face down
in the dirt
many times

unable to summon the strength to pick myself up -
not even the gods could have raised me from the dead
they had left me there to rot

there have been times
when my mouth could not open
sound could not escape
my cries for help
were silent screams echoing in the darkness
my body
had married the mud it lay in
and waited to be digested and absorbed
back into the womb of the earth

but right before my soul submitted
to the calls of my angels
and the joy of my demons
hands
held my wrists
waist
neck
back
and feet
lifting me out of the grave I had dug for myself
and propelling me into the warmth
of a midday sun

warmth which warmed those hands
wiped my eyes, cleared my vision
so I could see my path ahead

they placed me in healing waters
removing life's heavy debris with salt and flame
making my spirit balanced and whole again

they presented me to the four winds
reminding me that to feel was to live
and once I was dry and breathing again
naked and reborn
these hands
draped me in white cloth
clothed me in crystals and gems
and the wisdom of sages
an inheritance left for me in the libraries of the ancients
I was being put together again
made whole and fed with knowledge

these hands
placed swords in my palms
and taught me to fight against a world that sought to leave me in that mud
they gave me back my voice
fixed my crown
weaved gold thread into my locs
to remind me of my connection to the divine
and to every hand that reached out
and placed their hands in mine

these hands
which had saved my life
over and over
and over again

were the hands of sisters
daughters
aunts and cousins
maidens, mothers and crones

they are hands that belong to
artists and warriors
survivors and diviners
magicians
musicians
healers and dealers
they are queens and witches
femmes and b*tches
queers and wh*res
White and Black
whole and cracked
strangers, neighbors and friends

they are the daughters of Mother Earth

they are the hands
of Women

HUMAN

Human

they are human

humans who have been renamed as economic migrants
asylum seekers and refugees
labels lacking in care and compassion
painting pictures of people as less then deserving
so our governments can justify their hostility
casually discarding human beings as waste

human beings who their actions displaced

whose countries are being raped of natural resources
by forces too great for indigenous populations to fight
made victims of global corporate greed disguised as democracy
forcing generations to flee to unknown places
as brutal as the wars they barely escaped

places upheld as civilised on the western world's stage
despite failing to feed their own starving children
fund their own schools
and protect their own people's health
places governed by politicians who perform altruism
who serve their own private interests
line their designer pockets with public funds
and blame the lack of spending on those who come here
with nothing except the clothes on their backs
and the trauma still seeping from mangled skin

imagine

explaining your humanity to people who have none
repeating stories of how you went from being someone
to no one
to strange faces that scream hatred before stiffened lips part to speak
explaining to those proud of flags that boast of brutal 'conquests' of sky and sea
why you
a survivor of genocide
should be treated with dignity

these individuals decide who is migrant and who is human
it is not enough to have been robbed
of their homes, livelihoods and loved ones?
to have watched as soldiers stole their children's innocence?
to have had no choice but risk their new-borns life in the hope that they would save it
by sailing across channels and seas in packed, cheap dinghy's
pregnant with hope and hopelessness

to arrive on these so-called 'civilised' shores
having endured horrors we've only ever seen in films
met with hostility and abuse
told to go back to a home of rubble
berated for working jobs that people look down on
denied access to healthcare, shelter, education and cash
shamed and embarrassed for not speaking our language
left to survive on streets of the world's richest cities
and expected to feed a family on thirty-five pounds a week

the media would have us believe
that refugees don't give birth and don't bleed
their babies don't need milk, medicine, clothes or nappies
they don't feel pain, travel, socialise

and most certainly are not deserving of rights

will it take
for the wealthy to survive gas and bombs and rape
starvation, disease and red tape
to navigate killing fields for them to see
that their humanity can be stolen from them
as savagely as our government steals hope
when it creates refugees?
that we are all only one law away
from seeking asylum
from state sponsored violence and poverty?
these people our government damages indefinitely
aren't migrants, asylum seekers and refugees

Human

they are human
and it is the
fascists and racists in power
raised on hate and hypocrisy
that are soulless parasites
absent of humanity

HERE TO STAY (Written with Osman Yuzefzada)

Look at me

get used to my face
my thick and slender frame
my weird and wild ways
observe the many ways I display my femininity
and get used to what you see
listen to what I have to say
because whether you like it
or not

I am here to stay

my bhindis, locs and traditional frocks
mean more than a mere fashion statement
more than appropriated symbols of identity
they are more than part-time adornments of the privileged
they survived because I did
as you have a history of theft
you take and took from us
putting us on ships
shackling our hearts and minds
you enslaved my Ancestor for profit
except I am free

it makes me smile to see that in your ignorance
in the wearing of my culture
my heritage
my colours and symbols
my gifts and my curses
you are celebrating me

so copy
reinvent
try to obliterate who I am
but the truth is, and always will be

that I am here to stay

I have survived your famine
and now I fill my belly with love
I have survived your wars
and I've replaced them with my peace
I have survived your poverty
and am rich in spirit
I have survived your technologies
and transformed your weapons
from the gun and the sword
into the pen with which I write these words
words that will change the world

because I was taught that
you were better than me
that God is white, that God is male
that this God was chosen to rule over us
except I was born of a Woman
I grew in the womb
was nurtured by breasts
and it was she
that took my first breath

see
I am more than Kipling's 'white mans' burden'
I am more than the sum of my Ancestors labour
I am my language
I am my struggle

I am the glory of my heritage
despite the crimes of your colonialism
capitalism
patriarchy
and neoliberalism

I am still the perfume of Arabia
the silk of the Silk Route
the comfort of cotton
the kohl Black that lines the eyes of the beautiful
the strength in the tin pots you mock
I am the pride of your Britain
I built this place
and now you protect your statutes, your histories
but these are my histories of how I got here
and here I will remain
occupying spaces you said I had no right to be in

I will fight despite your insults
be that thug and looter you claim I am
and you will insist that I go back
where I once belonged
but I am here to stay

see my face
and remember my name
because I have, and always will
be here, to stay

FOR OLOKUN

How does one address your immense vastness and depth?

my prayers are but a drop
in an ocean so deep
that nobody alive has seen the fullness of its beauty

I come to you shrouded in humility
gratitude
my skin sweetened with the salt of my tears
I let them flow just as you do
making their way up from the depths of my soul
carrying with them treasured release
gifting me with a peace that could only be found where you reside

a part of me wishes to join you down there
to be nurtured and healed by you
to learn all the secrets of the Universe
to return to the primordial womb of this world
and be reborn as your child
reassured that life is as abundant as the treasures you keep concealed
and that I possess the strength to overcome all adversity
just as your waters overcome the earth

I know the water that flows through me belongs to you
which brings me comfort.
In solitude I contemplate our connection
listening with my heart
hoping you will share with me your ancient wisdom
praying that I am worthy enough to receive it

you have gifted me with a vision not of this world
I see the unseen, and hear Egguns voice in the silence
only you could have blessed me with such grace

and though it is not yet time for me
to gaze upon the beauty of your realm
I humbly and sincerely request
that you continue to guide and protect me
in whichever way you deem fit
and in return
I will honour you all ways

in thought
words
and deed

ensuring that those in your care are never forgotten
my children and those that follow will know your name
keeping your secrets for as long as life permits
until I am called back home

to you, Olokun

Printed in Great Britain
by Amazon